Drama for Students, Volume 1

STAFF

David Galens and Lynn M. Spampinato, *Editors*

Thomas Allbaugh, Craig Bentley, Terry Browne, Christopher Busiel, Stephen Coy, L. M. Domina, John Fiero, Carol L. Hamilton, Erika Kreger, Jennifer Lewin, Sheri Metzger, Daniel Moran, Terry Nienhuis, Bonnie Russell, Arnold Schmidt, William Wiles, Joanne Woolway, *Contributing Writers*

Elizabeth Cranston, Kathleen J. Edgar, Joshua Kondek, Marie Lazzari, Tom Ligotti, Marie Napierkowski, Scot Peacock, Mary Ruby, Diane Telgen, Patti Tippett, Kathleen Wilson, Pam Zuber, *Contributing Editors*

Pamela Wilwerth Aue, *Managing Editor*

Jeffery Chapman, *Programmer/Analyst*

Victoria B. Cariappa, *Research Team Manager*
Michele P. LaMeau, Andy Guy Malonis, Barb

ISSN applied for and pending
Printed in the United States of America
10 9 8 7 6 5 4 3

A Doll's House

Henrik Ibsen 1879

Introduction

A Doll's House was published on December 4, 1879, and first performed in Copenhagen on December 21, 1879. The work was considered a publishing event and the play's initial printing of 8,000 copies quickly sold out. The play was so controversial that Ibsen was forced to write a second ending that he called "a barbaric outrage" to be used only when necessary. The controversy centered around Nora's decision to abandon her children, and in the second ending she decides that the children need her more than she needs her freedom. Ibsen believed that women were best suited to be mothers and wives, but at the same time, he had an eye for injustice and Helmer's demeaning treatment of Nora was a common problem. Although he would later be embraced by feminists, Ibsen was no champion of women's rights; he only dealt with the problem of women's rights as a facet of the realism within his play. His intention was not to solve this issue but to illuminate it. Although Ibsen's depiction of Nora realistically illustrates the issues facing women, his decision in Act III to have her abandon her marriage and children was lambasted by critics as unrealistic, since, according to them, no "real" woman would ever make that choice. That Ibsen offered no real solution to Nora's dilemma inflamed critics and readers alike who were then left to debate the ending ceaselessly. This play established a new genre of modern drama; prior to *A Doll's House,* contemporary plays were usually historical romances or contrived comedy of manners. Ibsen is known as the "father of modern drama" because he elevated theatre from entertainment to a forum for exposing social problems. Ibsen broke away from the romantic tradition with his realistic portrayals of individual characters and his focus on psychological concerns as he sought to portray the real world, especially the position of women in society.

Ibsen was born March 20, 1828, in Skien, Norway, a lumbering town south of Christiania, now Oslo. He was the second son in a wealthy family that included five other siblings. In 1835, financial problems forced the family to move to a smaller house in Venstop outside Skien. After eight years the family moved back to Skein, and Ibsen moved to Grimstad to study as an apothecary's assistant. He applied to and was rejected at Christiania University. During the winter of 1848 Ibsen wrote his first play, *Catiline,* which was rejected by the Christiania Theatre; it was finally published in 1850 under the pseudonym Brynjolf Bjarme and generated little interest. Ibsen's second play, *The Burial Mound,* was also written under the pseudonym Brynjolf Bjarme, and became the first Ibsen play to be performed when it was presented on September 26, 1850, at the Christiania Theatre.

In 1851 Ibsen accepted an appointment as an assistant stage manager at the Norwegian Theatre in Bergen. He was also expected to assist the theatre as a dramatic author, and during his tenure at Bergen, Ibsen wrote *Lady Inger* (1855), *The Feast at Solhoug* (1856), and *Olaf Liljekrans* (1857). These early plays were written in verse and drawn from Norse folklore and myths. In 1857 Ibsen was released from his contract at Bergen and accepted a position at the Norwegian Theatre in Christiania. While there, Ibsen published *The Vikings at*

Helgeland and married Suzannah Thoresen in 1858. The couple's only child, Sigurd, was born the following year.

By 1860, Ibsen was under attack in the press for a lack of productivity—although he had published a few poems during this period. When the Christiania Theatre went bankrupt in 1862, Ibsen was left with no regular income except a temporary position as a literary advisor to the reorganized Christiania Theatre. Due to a series of small government grants, by 1863 Ibsen was able to travel in Europe and begin what became an intense period of creativity. During this period, Ibsen completed *The Pretenders* (1863) and a dramatic epic poem, "Brand" (1866), which achieved critical notice; these works were soon followed by *Peter Gynt* (1867). The first of Ibsen's prose dramas, *The League of Youth,* published in 1869, was also the first of his plays to demonstrate a shift from an emphasis on plot to one of interpersonal relationships. This was followed by *Emperor and Galilean* (1873), Ibsen's first work to be translated into English, and *Pillars of Society* (1877). *A Doll's House* (1879), *Ghosts* (1881), and *An Enemy of the People* (1882) are among the last plays included in Ibsen's realism period. Ibsen continued to write of modern realistic themes in his next plays, but he also relied increasingly on metaphor and symbolism in *The Wild Duck* (1884) and *Hedda Gabler* (1890).

A shift from social concerns to the isolation of the individual marks the next phase of Ibsen's work. *The Master Builder* (1892), *Little Eyolf* (1894),

John Gabriel Borkman (1896), and *When We Dead Awaken* (1899) all treat the conflicts that arise between art and life, between creativity and social expectations, and between personal contentment and self deception. These last works are considered by many critics to be autobiographical. In 1900, Ibsen suffered his first of several strokes. Ill health ended his writing career, and he died May 23, 1906.

Although Ibsen's audiences may have debated the social problems he depicted, modern critics are more often interested in the philosophical and psychological elements depicted in his plays and the ideological debates they generated.

Act I

The play opens on the day before Christmas. Nora returns home from shopping; although her husband is anticipating a promotion and raise, he still chides her excessive spending. In response, Nora flirts, pouts, and cajoles her husband as a child might, and, indeed, Torvald addresses her as he might a child. He hands her more money but only after having berating her spending. Their relationship parallels that of a daughter and father and, indeed, is exactly like the relationship Nora had with her father. Early in this act the audience is aware that the relationship between the Helmers is based on dishonesty when Nora denies that she has eaten macaroons, knowing that her husband has forbidden her to do so.

Nora is visited by an old friend, Kristine Linde. Mrs. Linde tells Nora that she has had some difficult problems and is seeking employment. Nora confesses to Mrs. Linde that she, too, has been desperate and recounts that she had been forced to borrow money several years earlier when her husband was ill. The money was necessary to finance a trip that saved her husband's life, but Nora forged her father's signature to secure the loan and lied to Torvald that her father had given them the money. Thus, she has been deceiving her husband for years as she worked to repay the loan. She tells this story to Mrs. Linde to demonstrate that she is an adult who is capable of both caring for her family and conducting business. Unfortunately, Nora's secret is shared by Krogstad, an employee at Torvald's bank. After a confrontation with Krogstad, Torvald decides to fire Krogstad and hire Mrs. Linde in his place.

Krogstad threatens Nora, telling her that if he loses his job he will reveal her earlier dishonesty. Krogstad fails to understand that Nora has no influence with her husband, nor does he appreciate the level of dishonesty that characterizes the Helmer marriage. For her part, Nora cannot believe that forging her father's signature-an act that saved her husband's life-could lead to a serious punishment. She cannot conceive that she could be held accountable and has an unrealistic appreciation for how the law and society functions. Still, she is concerned enough to plead Krogstad's cause with Torvald. Torvald refuses to reconsider firing Krogstad and forbids Nora to even mention his name.

Act II

Mrs. Linde stops by to help Nora prepare for a costume ball. Nora explains to Mrs. Linde that Krogstad is blackmailing her about the earlier loan. After Nora again begs Torvald not to fire Krogstad, her husband sends Krogstad an immediate notice of his dismissal. Nora is desperate and decides to ask help of Dr. Rank, a family friend. Before she can ask him for his help, Dr. Rank makes it obvious that he is in love with her and Nora determines that because of this it would be unwise to ask his help. Krogstad visits Nora once again and this time leaves a letter for Torvald in which Nora's dishonesty is revealed. To divert Torvald's attention from the mailbox, Nora elicits his help with her practice of the dance she is to perform, the tarantella. Finally, Nora asks Torvald to promise that he will not read the mail until after the party.

Act III

Krogstad had years earlier been in love with Mrs. Linde. At the beginning of this act they agree to marry, and Krogstad offers to retrieve his letter from Torvald. However, Mrs. Linde disagrees and thinks that it is time that Nora is forced to confront the dishonesty in her marriage. After the party, the Helmers return home and Torvald reads the letter from Krogstad. While Torvald reads in his study, Nora pictures herself as dead, having committed suicide by drowning in the icy river. Torvald interrupts her fantasy by demanding that she explain her deception. However, he refuses to listen and is only concerned with the damage to his own reputation. Torvald's focus on his own life and his lack of appreciation for the suffering undergone by Nora serve to open her eyes to her husband's faults. She had been expecting Torvald to rescue her and protect her, and instead he only condemns her and insists that she is not a fit mother to their children.

At that moment another letter arrives from Krogstad telling the Helmers that he will not take legal action against Nora. Torvald is immediately appeased and is willing to forget the entire episode. But having seen her husband revealed as a self-centered, selfish, hypocrite, Nora tells him that she can no longer live as a doll and expresses her intention to leave the house immediately. Torvald begs her to stay, but the play ends with Nora leaving the house, her husband, and her children.

Characters

Nora Helmer

Nora is the "doll" wife of Torvald. She is sensitive, sensible, and completely unaware of her own worth until the last act of the play. She initially appears flighty and excitable. Nora is most concerned with charming her husband and being the perfect wife; she is also secretive and hides her thoughts and actions from her husband even when there is no real benefit in doing so. Rather, deception appears to be almost a habit for Nora. Her husband constantly refers to her with pet names, such as "singing lark," "little squirrel," and "little spendthrift." He pats her on the head much as one would a favorite puppy. She forges her father's signature on a loan, lies to her husband about the source of the money, lies about how she spends the household accounts, and lies about odd jobs she takes to earn extra money. She is viewed as an object, a toy, a child, but never an equal. Her problem is that she is totally dependent upon her husband for all her needs; or she deceives herself into thinking so until the end of the play.

Torvald Helmer

Torvald is a smug lawyer and bank manager who represents a social structure that has decreed an inferior position for women. He is a symbol of society: male dominated, authoritative, and autocratic. He establishes rules for his wife, Nora. Some of the rules, such as no eating of macaroons, are petty and demeaning. He refers to his wife in the diminutive. She is always little, a plaything, a doll that must be occasionally indulged. He treats Nora just as her father did. Torvald has established a system of reward for Nora that responds to her subservient and childlike behaviors. If she flirts and wheedles and begs, he rewards her with whatever she asks. Torvald is critical of Nora when she practices her dance because he wants to keep her passion under control and he is concerned with propriety. He is completely unaware that Nora is capable of making serious decisions and is baffled at the play's conclusion when she announces that she is leaving him. He has failed to consider that she might have any serious needs or that her desires may contradict his own. Torvald is not a Neanderthal or a villain, but he often presents a challenge to students who can find little that is positive in his characterization.

Nils Krogstad

Krogstad is desperate and so initially he appears to be a villain; in fact, he has been trying to remake his life after having made earlier mistakes. He has also been disappointed in love and is bitter. His threats to Nora reflect his anger at being denied the opportunity to start over and his concerns about supporting his dependent children. Accordingly, he is not the unfeeling blackmailer he is presented as in the first act. Once he is reunited with his lost love, Mrs. Linde, he recants and attempts to rectify his earlier actions.

Kristine Linde

Mrs. Linde is a childhood friend of Nora's. She functions as the primary means by which the audience learns of Nora's secret. Mrs. Linde is a widow and quite desperate for work. At one time she was in love with Krogstad, but chose to marry for money so that she could provide support for her mother and younger brothers. At the end of the play, she and Krogstad are reconciled, but it is Mrs. Linde who decides that Nora and Torvald must face their problems. Thus, she stops Krogstad from retrieving his letter and moves the play toward its conclusion.

Media Adaptations

- *A Doll's House* was adapted for television for the first time in 1959. The adaptation starred Julie Harris, Christopher Plummer, Jason Robards, Hume Cronyn, Eileen Heckart, and Richard Thomas. Sonny Fox Productions. Available on videotape through MGM/UA Home Video, black and white, 89 minutes.

- *A Doll's House* was adapted for film for the second time in 1973. This version stars Jane Fonda, Edward Fox, Trevor Howard, and David Warner. The screenplay was by David Mercer. World Film services. Available on videotape through Prism Entertainment/Starmaker Entertainment, color, 98 minutes.

- *A Doll's House* was adapted for film again in 1977. This film stars Claire Bloom. Paramount Pictures.

- *A Doll's House* was adapted for film again in a 1989 Canadian production. Starring Claire Bloom, Anthony Hopkins, Ralph Richardson, Denholm Elliott, Anna Massey, and Edith Evans, this is considered a superior adaptation of the play. Elkins Productions Limited. Available on videotape through Hemdale Home Video, color, 96 minutes.

- *A Doll's House* was adapted for film most recently in 1991. This cast includes Juliet Stevenson, Trevor Eve, Geraldine James, Patrick Malahide, and David Calder. This is an excellent adaptation with some insightful commentaries by Alistair Cooke. PBS and BBC.

- In *A Doll's House, Part 1: The Destruction of Illusion,* Norris Houghton helps the audience explore the subsurface tensions of the play. Britannica Films, 1968.

- In *A Doll's House, Part II: Ibsen's Themes,* Norris Houghton examines the characters and the themes of the play. Britannica Films, 1968.

- *A Doll's House,* audio recording, 3 cassettes. With Claire Bloom and Donald Madden. Caedmon/Harper Audio.

Dr. Rank

Dr. Rank is a family friend of the Helmers, who is secretly in love with Nora. Dr. Rank has been affected by his father's corruption; he suffers from syphilis inherited from his father and he is dying. When Nora finally realizes that Rank loves her, she decides that she cannot ask him for help. Rank's treatment of Nora contrasts sharply with Torvald's. Rank always treats Nora like an adult. He listens to her and affords her a dignity missing in Torvald's treatment. He tells Nora that when he is near death he will send her a card. It arrives in the same mail as Krogstad's letter and receives little attention in the ensuing melee.

Themes

Nora Helmer, the "doll" wife, realizes after eight years of marriage that she has never been a partner in her marriage. At the play's conclusion, she leaves her husband in order to establish an identity for herself that is separate from her identity as a wife and mother.

Appearances and Reality

On the surface, Nora Helmer appears to be the ideal wife her husband desires. Torvald sees a woman who is under his control; he defines her every behavior and establishes rules that govern everything from what she eats to what she buys. The reality is that Nora has been maintaining a secret life for seven years, and that Torvald and Nora maintain a marriage that is a fiction of suitability and trust. Torvald has a public persona to maintain and he views his marriage as an element of that public need. When the fiction is stripped away at the play's conclusion, both partners must confront the reality of their marriage.

Topics for Further Study

- Feminists are often bothered by the reconciliation between Kristine and Krogstad. Just as Nora is breaking free of the confines of her marriage, Kristine is embracing marriage. Do you agree with some feminists critics that Kristine's decision to reunite with Krogstad negates Nora's flight to personal freedom? Investigate the role of women in late nineteenth-century marriage and compare the two different ways that Nora and Kristine seek to define their identity within the social convention of marital life.

- In a second ending that Ibsen was forced to write, Nora looks at her sleeping children and realizes that she cannot leave them. Instead of seeking her freedom and discovering her identity, she decides to remain in the marriage. Compare the two endings offered for this play. Given the social and cultural context in which the play is set, which ending do you think best reflects the realities of nineteenth-century European life?

- The Helmer's marriage can best be described as a marriage of deception. Torvald has no idea who Nora really is and is in love with the wife he thinks he possesses. Nora is also in love with a vision rather than reality. During the course of the play, these deceptions are stripped away and each sees the other as if for the first time. The audience also sees the reality of Victorian life. The ideal family and house, the decorated tree and the festivities of the holidays also perpetuate the Victorian myth; but is it a myth? Investigate the economic and social conditions of the nineteenth century. Charles Dickens's view of this society predates Ibsen's by less than half a century, and yet Dickens's view of the social condition is often regarded as especially bleak and pessimistic. Would you agree or is the artificiality of the Helmer household just as bleak as that outlined in any Dickens novel?

Betrayal

Betrayal becomes a theme of this play in several ways. Nora has betrayed her husband's trust in several instances. She has lied about borrowing money, and to repay the money she must lie about how she spends her household accounts and she must lie about taking odd jobs to earn extra money. But she also chooses to lie about eating sweets her husband has forbidden her. However, Nora trusts in Torvald to be loyal to her and, in the end, he betrays that trust when he rejects her pleas for understanding. Torvald's betrayal of her love is the impetus that Nora requires to finally awaken to her own needs.

Deception

Deception is an important theme in *A Doll's House* because it motivates Nora's behavior, and through her, the behavior of every other character in the play. Because Nora lied when she borrowed money from Krogstad, she must continue lying to repay the money. But, Nora thinks she must also lie to protect Torvald. Her deception makes her vulnerable to Krogstad's blackmail and casts him in the role of villain. And although Nora does not lie to Mrs. Linde, it is Mrs. Linde who forces Nora to confront her deceptions. Dr. Rank has been deceiving both Nora and Torvald for years about the depth of his feelings for Nora. Only when she attempts to seek his help does Nora finally see beneath the surface to the doctor's real feelings. Torvald, who has been deceived throughout most of the play, is finally revealed in the final act to have been the one most guilty of deception, since he has deceived Nora into believing that he loved and cherished her, while all the while he had regarded her as little more than his property.

Growth and Development

In Act I, Nora is little more than a child playing a role; she is a "doll" occupying a doll's house, a child who has exchanged a father for a husband without changing or maturing in any way. Nevertheless, through the course of the play she is finally forced to confront the reality of the life she is living. Nora realizes in the final act of A *Doll's House* that if she wants the opportunity to develop an identity as an adult that she must leave her husband's home. When Nora finally gives up her dream for a miracle and, instead, accepts the reality of her husband's failings, she finally takes her first steps toward maturity.

Honor

Honor is of overwhelming importance to Torvald; it is what motivates his behavior. Early in the play, Torvald's insistence on the importance of honor is the reason he offers for firing Krogstad, asserting that because he once displayed a lack of honor means that Krogstad is forever dishonored. When he learns of his wife's mistake, Torvald's first and foremost concern is for his honor. He cannot appreciate the torment or sacrifice that Nora has made for him because he can only focus on how society will react to his family's shame. For Torvald, honor is more important than family and far more important than love; he simply cannot conceive of anyone placing love before honor. This issue exemplifies the crucial difference between Nora and Torvald.

Identity and Search for Self

In the final act of *A Doll's House,* Nora is forced to acknowledge that she has no identity separate from that of her husband. This parallels the reality of nineteenth century Europe where a wife was regarded as property rather than partner. Torvald owns Nora just as he owns their home or any other possession. Her realization of this in the play's final act provides the motivation she needs to leave her husband. When Nora realizes the inequity of her situation, she also recognizes her own self worth. Her decision to leave is a daring one that indicates the seriousness of Nora's desire to find and create her own identity.

Pride

Like honor, pride is an important element in how Torvald defines himself. He is proud of Nora in the same way one is proud of an expensive or rare possession. When her failing threatens to become public knowledge, Torvald is primarily concerned with the loss of public pride. Nora's error reflects on his own sense of perfection and indicates to him an inability to control his wife. Rather than accept Nora as less than perfect, Torvald instead rejects her when she is most in need of his support. His pride in himself and in his possessions blinds him to Nora's worth. Because she has always believed in Torvald's perfection, Nora is at first also unaware of her own strengths. Only when she has made the decision to leave Torvald can Nora begin to develop pride in herself.

Sexism

Sexism as a theme is reflected in the disparate lives represented in this play. Nora's problems arise because as a woman she cannot conduct business without the authority of either her father or her husband. When her father is dying, she must forge his signature to secure a loan to save her husband's life. That she is a responsible person is demonstrated when she repays the loan at great personal sacrifice. In the nineteenth century women's lives were limited to socially prescribed behaviors, and women were considered to be little more than property; Nora embodies the issues that confronted women during this period. Torvald's injustice cannot be ignored and Nora's sympathetic loss of innocence is too poignant to be forgotten. Thus, the controversy surrounding sexual equality becomes an important part of the play.

Style

This is a three act play with prose dialogue, stage directions, and no interior dialogue. There are no soliloquies, and thus, the thoughts of the characters and any action off stage must be explained by the actors. The actors address one another in *A Doll's House* and not the audience.

Acts

Acts comprise the major divisions within a drama. In Greek plays the sections of the drama were signified by the appearance of the chorus and were usually divided into five acts. This is the formula for most serious drama from the Greeks to the Romans, and to Elizabethan playwrights like William Shakespeare. The five acts denote the structure of dramatic action; they are exposition, complication, climax, falling action, and catastrophe. The five act structure was followed until the nineteenth century when Ibsen combined some of the acts. *A Doll's House* is a three act play; the exposition and complication are combined in the first act when the audience learns of both Nora's deception and of the threat Krogstad represents. The climax occurs in the second act when Krogstad again confronts Nora and leaves the letter for Torvald to read. The falling action and catastrophe are combined in Act Three when Mrs. Linde and Krogstad are reconciled but Mrs. Linde decides to let the drama play itself out and Torvald reads and reacts to the letter with disastrous results.

Naturalism

Naturalism was a literary movement of the late nineteenth and early twentieth centuries, and is the application of scientific principles to literature. For instance, in nature behavior is determined by environmental pressures or internal factors, none of which can be controlled or even clearly understood. There is a clear cause and effect association: either the indifference of nature or biological determinism influences behavior. In either case, there is no human responsibility for the actions of the individual. European Naturalism emphasized biological determinism, while American Naturalism emphasized environmental influences. Thus, Torvald's accusation that all of her father's weakest moral values are displayed in Nora is based on an understanding that she has inherited those traits from him.

Realism

Realism is a nineteenth century literary term that identifies an author's attempt to portray characters, events, and settings in a realistic way. Simply put, realism is attention to detail, with description intended to be honest and frank at all levels. There is an emphasis on character, especially behavior. Thus, in *A Doll's House,* the events of the Helmers's marriage are easily recognizable as realistic to the audience. These are events, people, and a home that might be familiar to any person in the audience. The sitting room is similar to one found in any other home. Nora is similar to any other wife in nineteenth-century Norway, and the problems she encounters in her marriage are similar to those confronted by other married women.

Setting

The time, place, and culture in which the action of the play takes place is called the setting. The elements of setting may include geographic location, physical or mental environments, prevailing cultural attitudes, or the historical time in which the action takes place. The location for *A Doll's House* is an unnamed city in nineteenth-century Norway. The action begins just before Christmas and concludes the next evening, and all three acts take place in the same sitting room at the Helmers's residence. The Helmers have been married for eight years; Nora is a wife and mother, and her husband, Torvald, is a newly promoted lawyer and bank manager. They live in comfortable circumstances during a period that finds women suppressed by a social system that equates males with success in the public sphere and females with domestic chores in the private sphere. But this is also a period of turmoil as women demand greater educational opportunities and greater equality in the business world. Accordingly, *A Doll's House* illuminates many of the conflicts and questions being debated in nineteenth-century Europe.

Women's Rights

In 1888, married women in Norway were finally given control over their own money, but the Norway of Ibsen's play pre-dates this change and provides a more restrictive environment for women such as Nora Helmer. In 1879, a wife was not legally permitted to borrow money without her husband's consent, and so Nora must resort to deception to borrow the money she so desperately needs. Ibsen always denied that he believed in women's rights, stating instead that he believed in human rights.

Compare & Contrast

- **1879:** Congress gives women the right to practice law before the United States Supreme Court.

  Today: Women attorneys are as common as men in all areas of the law. Acceptance for women in the upper echelons of corporate law proved to be a bigger hurdle than practicing before the Supreme Court. Despite all of the advances made in the area of gender equality, women still earn less than seventy cents for every dollar earned by men.

- **1879:** Edison announces the success of his incandescent light bulb, certain that it will burn for 100 hours. Arc-lights are installed as streetlights in San Francisco and Cleveland.

  Today: Electric lights illuminate theatres, businesses, and homes in all areas of the industrialized world and have become a part of the human environment that is so accepted as to go largely unnoticed and often unappreciated.

- **1879:** In Berlin, electricity drives a railroad locomotive for the first time. George Seldon files for a patent for a road vehicle to be powered by an internal combustion engine.

  Today: Transportation based on the earlier combustion engine has been greatly refined and is easy, accessible, and fast. But it is only now that electricity is being researched seriously as a power source for more ecologically prudent transportation.

- **1879:** A woman's college, Radcliffe, is founded by Elizabeth Cary

Agassiz in Cambridge, Massachusetts.

Today: The opportunity for an education has ceased to be a novelty for women in the United States and most of Europe. Yet even in the late 1990s legal battles are waged over a woman's right to enter a male-only federally subsidized school, the Citadel.

- **1879:** The multiple switchboard invented by Leroy B. Firman is invented; it will help make the telephone a commercial success and dramatically increase the number of telephone subscribers.

Today: Telephone lines are no longer used only for transmitting conversations, as communications have expanded to include computers and multimedia technology. The video phone and computers that permit visual connection in addition to vocal are now a reality and will likely become common and more affordable for much of the industrialized world.

The issue of women's rights was already a force in Norway several years before Ibsen focused on the issue, and women had been the force behind several changes. Norway was a newly liberated country in the nineteenth century, having been freed from Danish control in 1814; therefore, it is understandable that issues involving freedom—both political and personal freedom—were important in the minds of Norwegians. Poverty had already forced women into the workplace early in the nineteenth century, and the Norwegian government had passed laws protecting and governing women's employment nearly five decades before Ibsen's play. By the middle of the century women were granted the same legal protection as that provided to male children. Women were permitted inheritance rights and were to be successful in petitioning for the right to a university education only three years after the first performance of *A Doll's House*. But many of the protections provided to women were aimed at the lower economic classes. Employment opportunities for women were limited to low-paying domestic jobs, teaching, or clerical work. Middle-class women, such as Nora, noticed few of these new advantages. It was the institution of marriage itself that restricted the freedom of middle-class women. Although divorce was available and inexpensive, it was still socially stigmatized and available only if both partners agreed. The play's ending makes clear that Torvald would object to divorce and so Nora's alienation from society would be even greater. There was no organized feminist movement operating in Norway in 1879. Thus Nora's exodus at the play's conclusion is a particularly brave and dangerous act. There was no army of feminist revolutionaries to protect and guide her; she was completely alone in trying to establish a new life for herself.

Christmas Celebrations

Christmas was an important family holiday in Norway and was viewed as a time of family unity and celebration. Thus it is ironic that the play opens on Christmas Eve and that the Helmer family unity disintegrates on Christmas Day. Christmas Day and the days following were traditionally reserved for socializing and visiting with neighbors and friends. Costume parties such as the one Nora and Torvald attend were common, and the dance Nora performs, the tarantella, is a dance for couples or for a line of partners. That Nora dances it alone signifies her isolation both within her marriage and in the community.

Sources

Nora's forgery is similar to one that occurred earlier in Norway and one with which Ibsen was personally connected. A woman with whom Ibsen was friendly, Laura Kieler, borrowed money to finance a trip that would repair her husband's health. When the loan came due, Kieler was unable to repay it. She tried to raise money by selling a manuscript she had written and Ibsen, feeling the manuscript was inferior, declined to help her get it published. In desperation, Kieler forged a check, was caught, and was rejected by her husband who then sought to gain custody of their children and have his wife committed to an asylum. After her release, Kieler pleaded with her husband to take her back, which he did rather unwillingly. Ibsen provides Nora with greater resilience and ingenuity than that evidenced by Kieler. Nora is able to earn the money to repay the loan, and her forgery is of her father's signature on a promissory note and not of a check. Lastly, Nora is saved by Krogstad's withdrawal of legal threats and so is not cast out by her husband. Instead, she becomes stronger and her husband is placed in the position of the marital partner who must plead for a second chance. Ibsen provides a careful reversal of the original story that strengthens the character of the "doll" wife.

Critical Overview

In Norway, *A Doll's House* was published two weeks before its first performance. The initial 8,000 copies of the play sold out immediately and so the audience for the play was both informed, excited, and eagerly anticipating the play's first production. The play elicited much debate, most of it centered on Nora's decision to leave her marriage at the play's conclusion. Reaction in Germany was similar to that in Norway. Ibsen was forced to provide an alternative ending by the management of its first German production, since even the actress playing Nora refused to portray a mother leaving her children in such a manner. Ibsen called the new ending, which had Nora abandoning her plans to leave upon seeing her children one last time, "a barbaric outrage to be used only in emergencies." The debate was focused not on women's rights or other feminist issues such as subordination or male dominance; instead, people were consumed with the question, "What kind of a wife and mother would walk out on her family as Nora does?" The play's reception elsewhere in Europe mirrored that of Norway and Germany with the debate still focused largely on social issues and not on the play's challenge to dramatic style.

Another issue for early reviewers was Nora's transformation. Many critics simply did not accept the idea that the seemingly submissive, flighty woman of the first two acts could display so much resolve and strength in the third act. According to Errol Durbach in *A Doll's House: Ibsen's Myth of Transformation,* one review of the period stated that Ibsen had disgusted his audience by "violating the unconventional." Many reviewers just could not visualize any woman displaying the kind of behavior demonstrated by Nora. It was beyond their comprehension that a woman would voluntarily choose to sacrifice her children in order to seek her own identity. Durbach argued that the audience and the critics were accustomed to social problem plays, but that Ibsen's play presented a problem without the benefit of a ready or acceptable solution. In fact, the critics identified with Torvald and saw his choice of so unstable a wife as Nora as his only real flaw. In 1879 Europe, *A Doll's House* was a problem play, but not the one Ibsen envisioned. Instead, the problem resided with the critics who were so consumed with the issue of Nora's decision that they ignored the deeper complexities of the play. Early in the first act it becomes clear that Nora has a strength and determination that even she cannot acknowledge. When her eyes are opened in Act III, it is not so much a metamorphosis as it is an awakening.

In England, the play was embraced by Marxists who envisioned an egalitarian mating without the hierarchy of marriage and an end to serfdom when wives ceased to be property. But many other Englishmen were more interested in the aesthetics of the play than in its social content. Bernard Shaw embraced Ibsen's dramatic poetry and championed the playwright's work. Since the first performance of A *Doll's House* in England occurred ten years after its debut in Norway, the English were provided with more time to absorb the ideas presented in the play. Thus the reviews of the period lacked the vehemence of those in Norway and Germany. Rather, according to Durbach, Ibsen was transformed into a liberal championed by English critics more interested in his dramatic poetry than the nature of his argument. In her 1919 book, *Ibsen in England,* Miriam Alice Franc declared that Ibsen "swept from the stage the false sentimentality and moral shams that had reigned there. He emancipated the theatre from the thraldom of convention."

Initial responses in America were even less enthusiastic then in Europe. Many critics dismissed Ibsen as gloomy and pessimistic and as representing the "old world." But by 1905, a production starring Ethel Barrymore was embraced by early feminists. Durbach noted that Barry more's performance occurred within the context of the American woman's efforts at emancipation, and Ibsen became an "Interpreter of American Life." In his introduction to *The Collected Works of Henrik Ibsen,* which was published between 1906 and 1912, William Archer remarked: "It is with *A Doll's House* that Ibsen enters upon his kingdom as a world-poet." Archer added that this play was the work that would carry Ibsen's name beyond Norway. In a 1986 performance review, *New York Times* contributor Walter Goodman declared that A *Doll's House* is "a great document of feminism, and Nora is an icon of women's liberation."

What Do I Read Next?

- Joyce Carol Oates's short story, "The Lady With The Pet Dog," offers an interesting contrast to the way Nora chooses to deal with her marriage. This is the retelling of the Chekhov story, only from the woman's point of view. The theme of deception is also important in this story, since Anna chooses to keep secret important events in her life. Her efforts to escape her marriage and establish a new identity are different from Nora's because she internalizes the changes and so is not forced to confront her husband in the same manner that Nora must.

- In both William Shakespeare's *Hamlet* and Henrik Ibsen's A *Doll's*

House, there is a huge disparity between image and reality. If a character is known by what he/she says or he/she does or by what others say about him/her, then both these plays offer interesting opportunities to compare how the differing perspectives of personality affect the outcome of each play.

- Susan Glaspell's *Trifles* was written almost forty years after *A Doll's House*. In Glaspell's play, the relationship between men and women is certainly as oppressive as in Ibsen's. The differences in setting, notably the dirt and poverty of the Wrights' home, serve as an interesting contrast to the decor of the Helmers'. Still, the female inhabitants face similar struggles and Mrs. Wright's chosen method of escape offers an interesting opposition to Nora's.

- James Joyce's short story "The Dead" can be compared to Ibsen's *A Doll's House*. Both depict a woman's struggle to become emotionally independent of the husband who seeks to control her. In both cases, there are secrets and deception involved in the wife's past. Both also feature Christmas as a background for some of the play's events.

- In Ibsen's *Ghosts,* the author further explores the ramifications of a father's actions on his family. As in *A Doll's House,* this play embraces naturalism as an explanation for human behavior. In the play, the sins of the father become manifest in the son when the son discovers he has inherited his father's venereal disease and that he is in love with his illegitimate half-sister. In *A Doll's House,* Dr. Rank, too, inherits the venereal disease of his father.

Further Reading

Magill, Frank N., editor. *Masterpieces of World Literature,* Harper & Row, 1989, pp. 203-206.

> This book compresses literary works into easily understood summaries. In addition to plot summaries and character reviews, the editor also addresses historical context and critical interpretations. The Magill compilations provide a reliable, accessible means for students to review texts.

Meyer, Michael, editor. *The Compact Bedford Introduction to Literature,* 4th Edition, St. Martin's Press, 1996, pp. 1128-1136.

> This anthology encapsulates several brief approaches to the study of this play. Excerpts from psychological, Marxist, and feminists readings are provided to assist students with a comparison of the different critical readings possible.

Rickert, Blandine M., editor. *Major Modern Dramatists,* Volume 2, pp. 1-32.

> This work provides an introduction to Ibsen drawn from reviews and critical interpretations of his work. Excerpts date from late in the

nineteenth century to the late twentieth century. Compiling this information allows students of Ibsen to see how his plays have influenced succeeding generations.

Sources

Archer, William. Introduction to *The Collected Works of Henrik Ibsen,* edited and translated by Archer, Scribner, 1906-1912.

Durbach, Errol. *A Doll's House: Ibsen's Myth of Transformation,* Twayne Masterworks Studies, Twayne Publishers, 1991.

Finney, Gail. "Ibsen and Feminism," in *The Cambridge Companion to Ibsen,* edited by James McFarlane, Cambridge University Press, 1994, pp. 89-105.

Franc, Miriam Alice. *Ibsen in England,* The Four Seas Co., 1919, pp. 131-33.

Goodman, Walter. Review of *A Doll's House, The New York Times,* May 14, 1986.

Hemmer, Bjorn. "Ibsen and the Realistic Problem Drama," in *The Cambridge Companion to Ibsen,* edited by James McFarlane, Cambridge University Press, 1994, pp. 68-88.